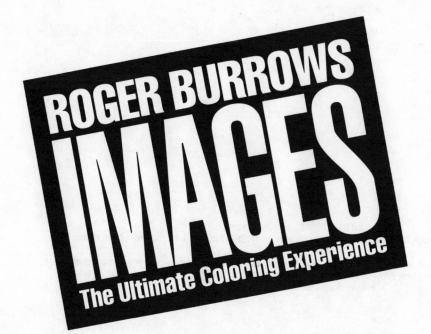

ROGER BURROWS
IMAGES
The Ultimate Coloring Experience

RUNNING PRESS
PHILADELPHIA · LONDON

30 29 28 27
Digit on the right indicates the number of this printing.

ISBN 1–56138–109–8

Cover design by Toby Schmidt
Interior design by Christian Benton
Typography: Helvetica Compressed by Commcor Communications, Philadelphia, Pennsylvania
Front and back cover artwork by Barney Schmidt
Back cover artwork by Lili Schwartz and Jon Pochos

This book may be ordered by mail from the publisher.
Please add $2.50 for postage and handling.
But try your bookstore first!
Running Press Book Publishers
125 South Twenty-second Street
Philadelphia, Pennsylvania 19103–4399

INTRODUCTION

Begin by looking at the designs—<u>really</u> looking at them. But don't strain your eyes. Just relax.

Most people see shapes and patterns at first, and then many start to see pictures, objects, faces, animals, and other forms. Some see entire scenes with birds, trees, and buildings. Once you see a shape or an object, you can change it by adding or subtracting other elements within the design. Coloring the designs enhances this process and also serves to fix the image that you have seen—and of course what you have seen becomes visible to others.

The idea for <u>Images</u> designs goes back to the early '70s. At that time I was a teacher and lecturer in mathematics and geometry as well as an art teacher, and I developed a dynamic new geometry based on "close packing" circles and spheres. Close packing is something that happens when you put three circles together. For example, if you group three dimes together, they'll form a triangle. If you continue to add dimes, the triangular pattern will continue infinitely. Close packing is a very efficient way to put things together. Natural examples can be found in everything from beehives to atoms.

The new geometry generated unusual "close packing" arrangements of different sized circles. I took some of these arrangements and connected the centers of the circles. The resulting designs were published under the name <u>Clopac</u> around 1971. Many more designs resulted from arduously hand-drawing lines in and around the close packing circles: tangents, chords, radii, stars. With this, <u>Images</u> designs were born.

Life is much easier now: all of the designs in this book have been produced on my portable Apple Macintosh. If only I had had it in the early '70s!

I freely and gratefully acknowledge the encouragement and support of my friends and colleagues during the period of creating the new geometry: Dr. Ensor Holiday, a remarkable man whose fascination with geometry inspired him to produce the <u>Altair</u> <u>Design</u> books; Michael Holt, author and creative mathematician, who helped me think about what I was doing; Francis Huxley, author and nephew of Aldous Huxley, who provided support and encouraged me to explore the cultural development and use of geometrical forms; and many others too numerous to mention.

Roger Burrows is the author of twenty books and papers on geometry, design, and architectural form, and more than fifty books for children. In the early '70s he worked with Dr. Ensor Holiday, of Guys Hospital, London, to develop Altair Designs, which were variations of a particular geometrical pattern from a collection of architectural designs assembled during Napoleon's occupation of Egypt.

Mr. Burrows is currently a publishing executive with John B. Fairfax International and is based in New York. Prior to that he developed Questron, an interactive book and electronic "wand" system for children. He has also designed a number of major exhibitions in the United Kingdom, including an exhibition of futuristic designs for the investiture of the Prince of Wales, and geometrical structures for the Architectural Association in London.

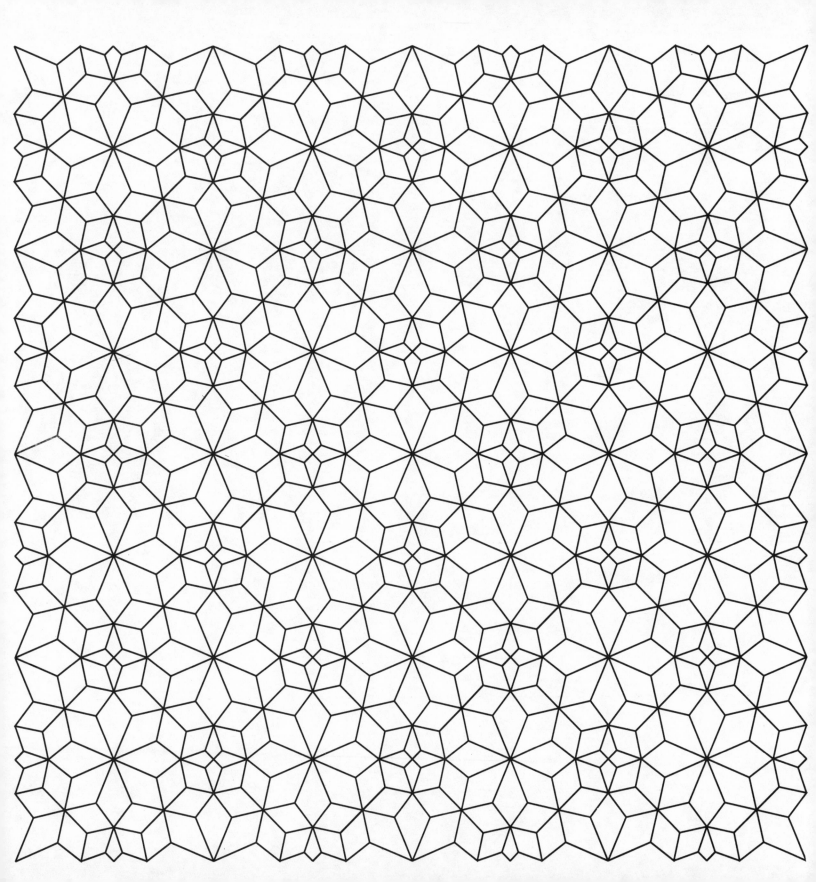

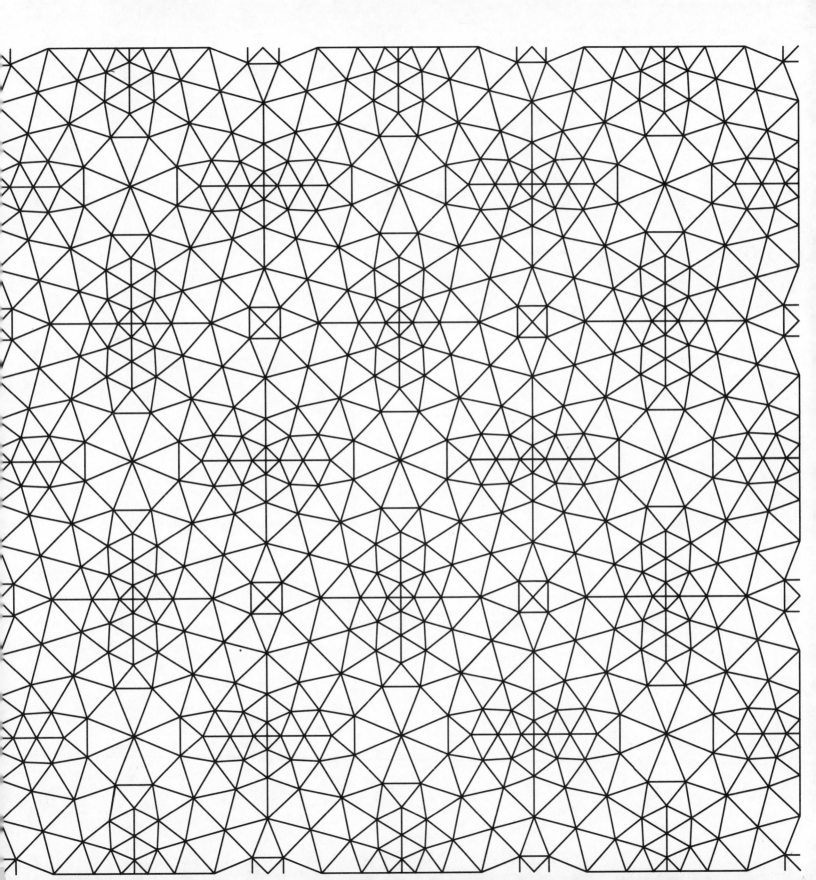

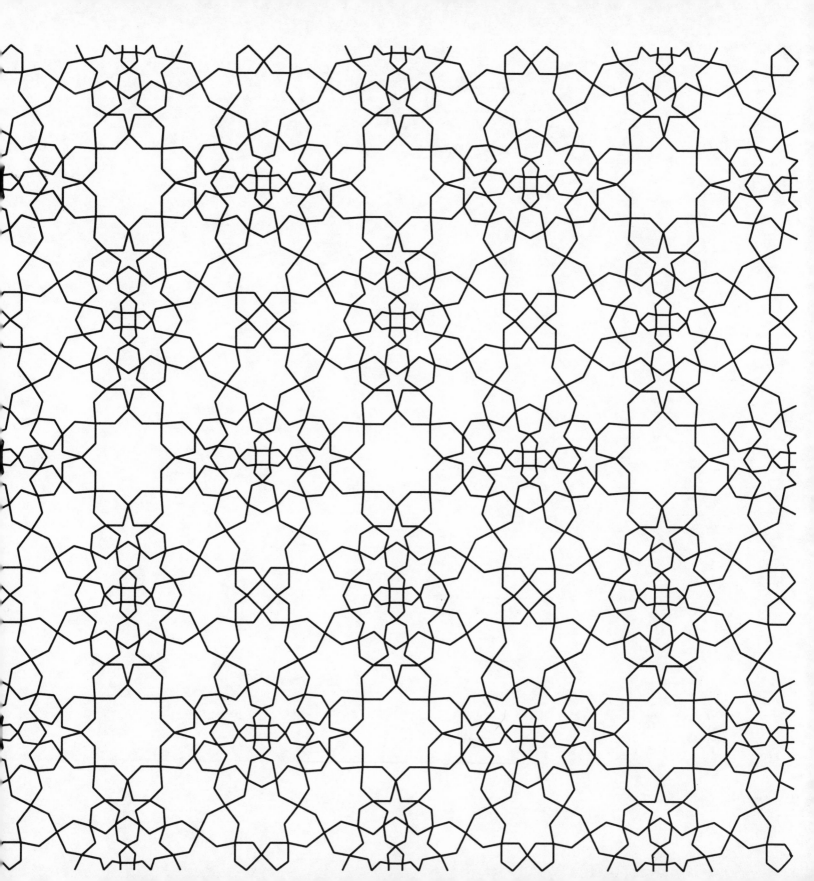

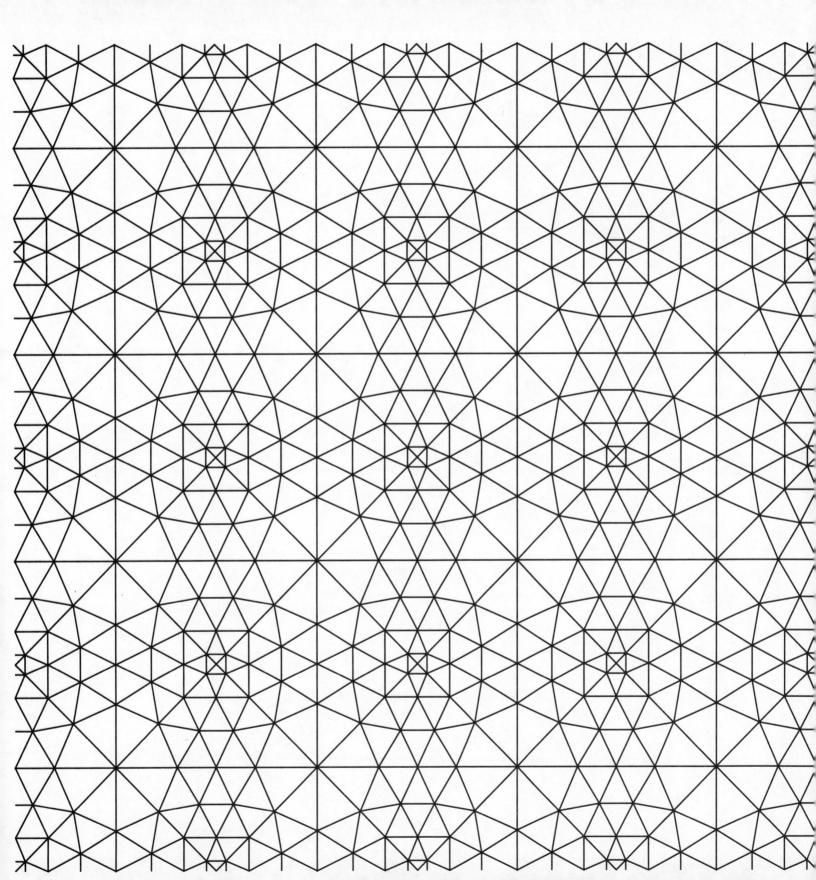

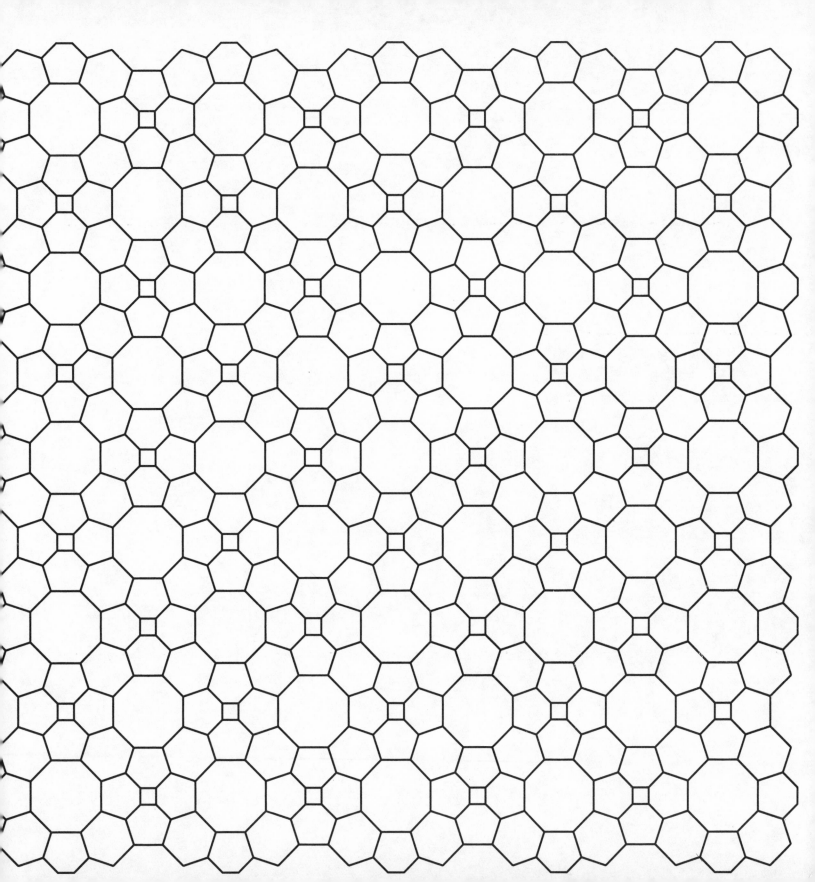

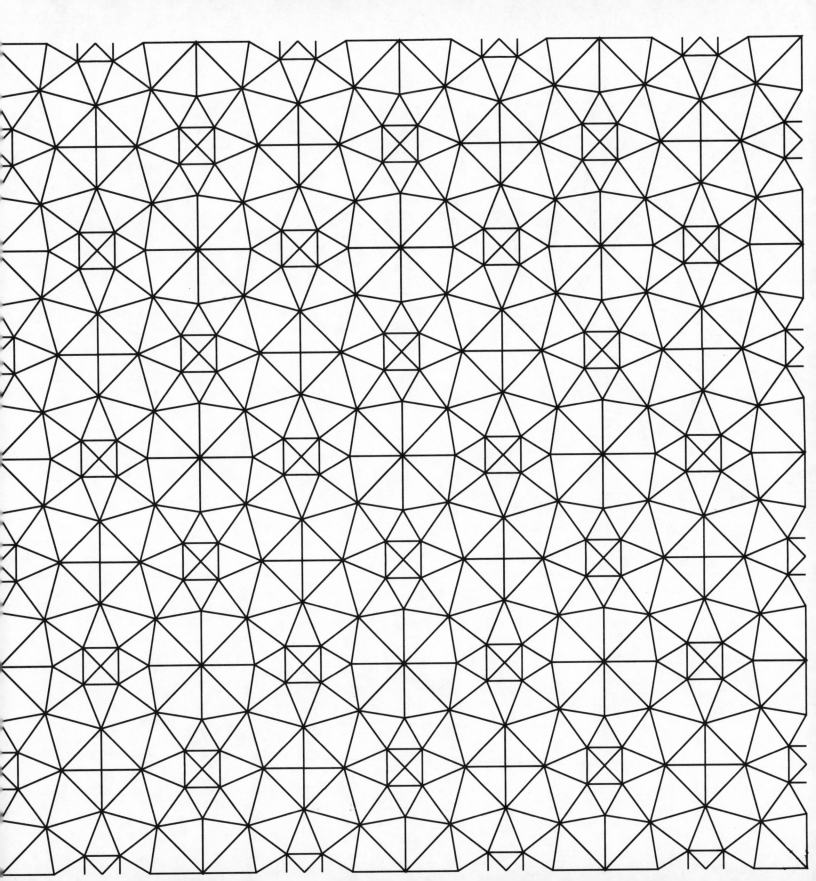

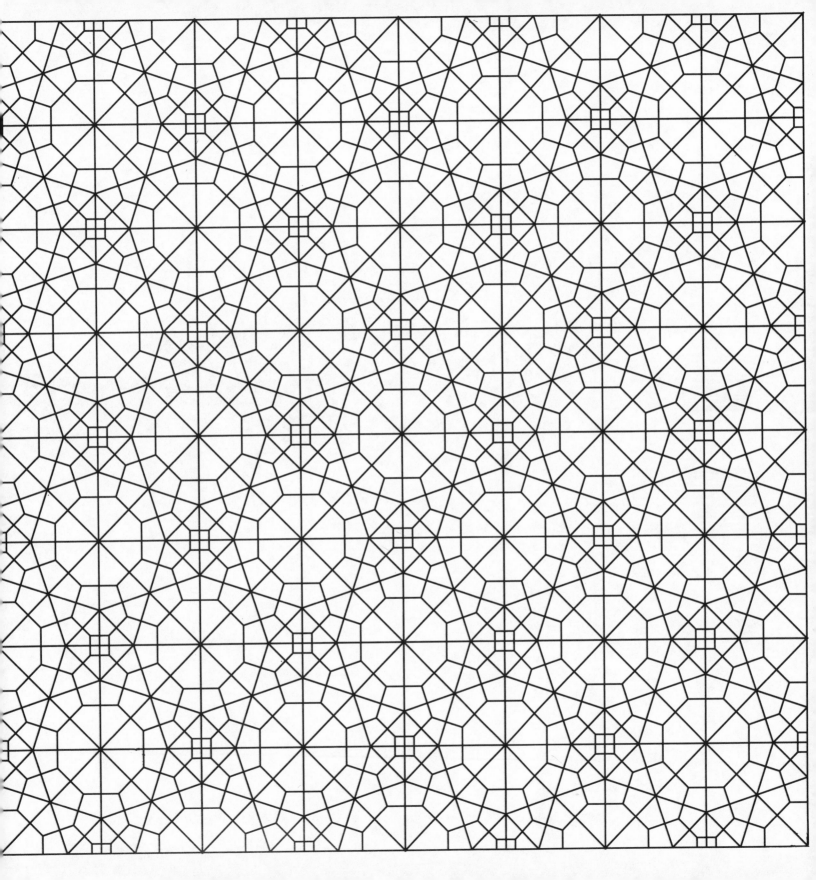

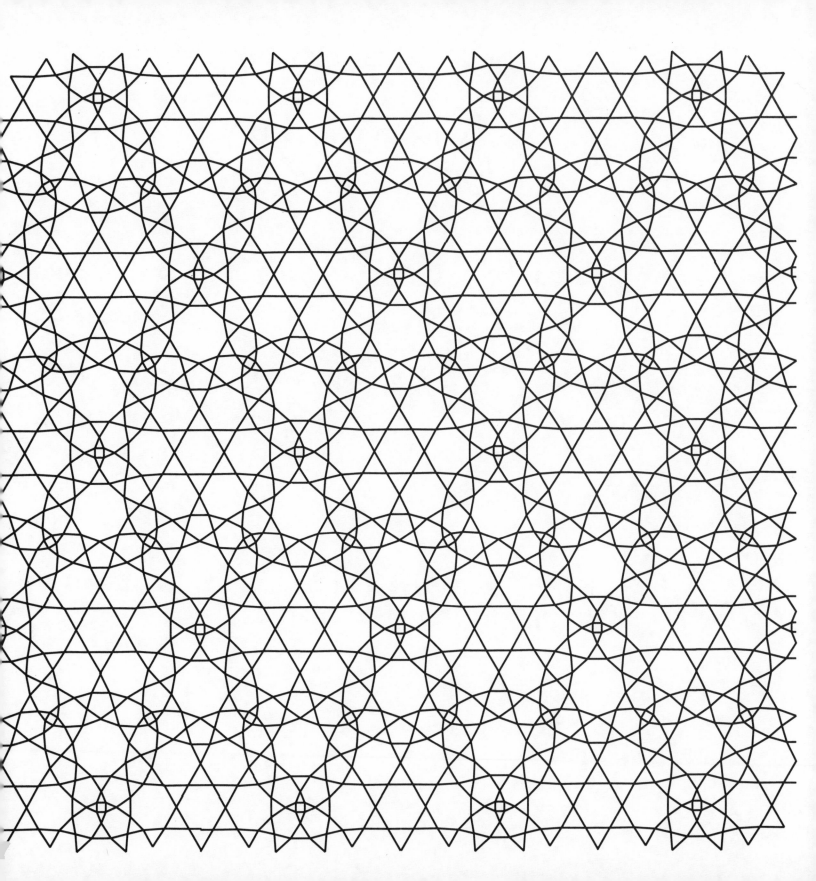

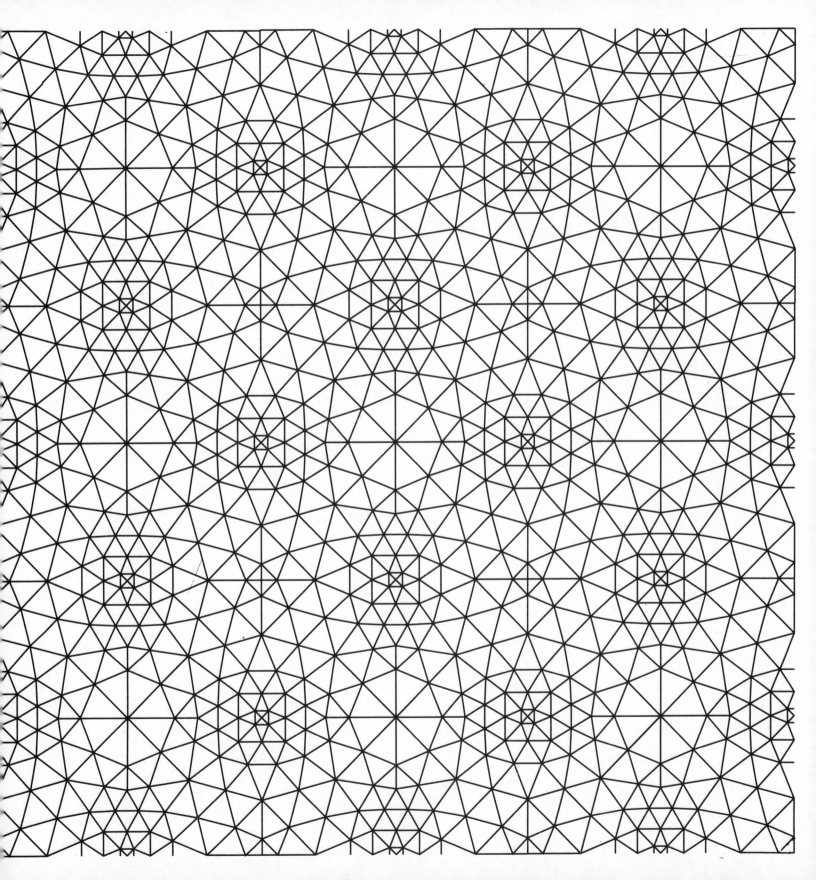

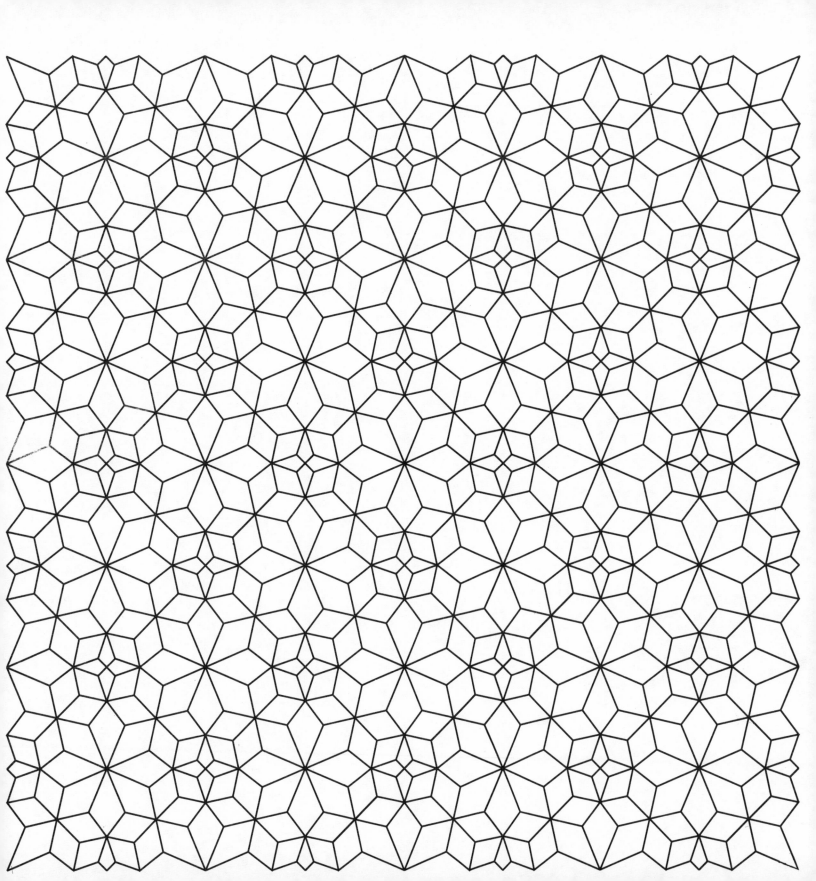

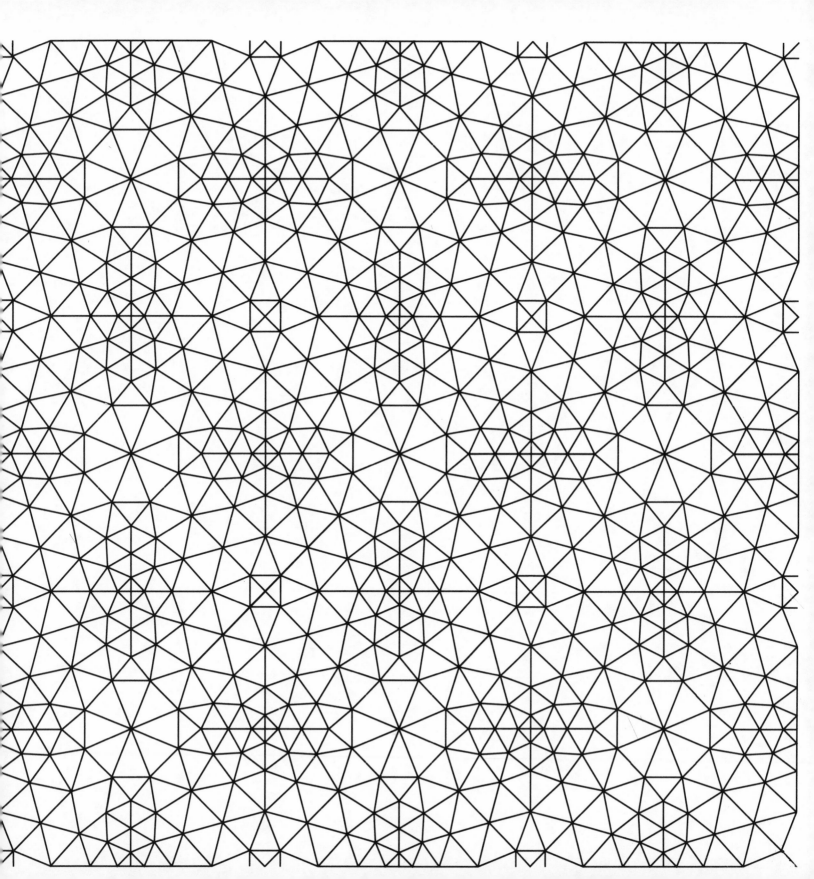

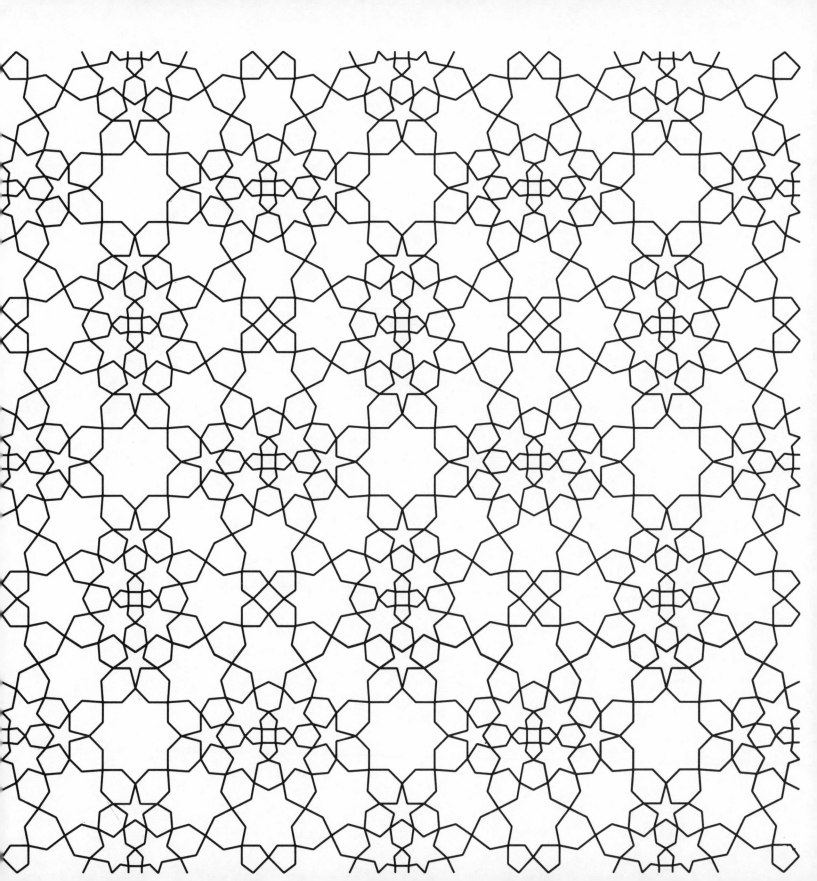

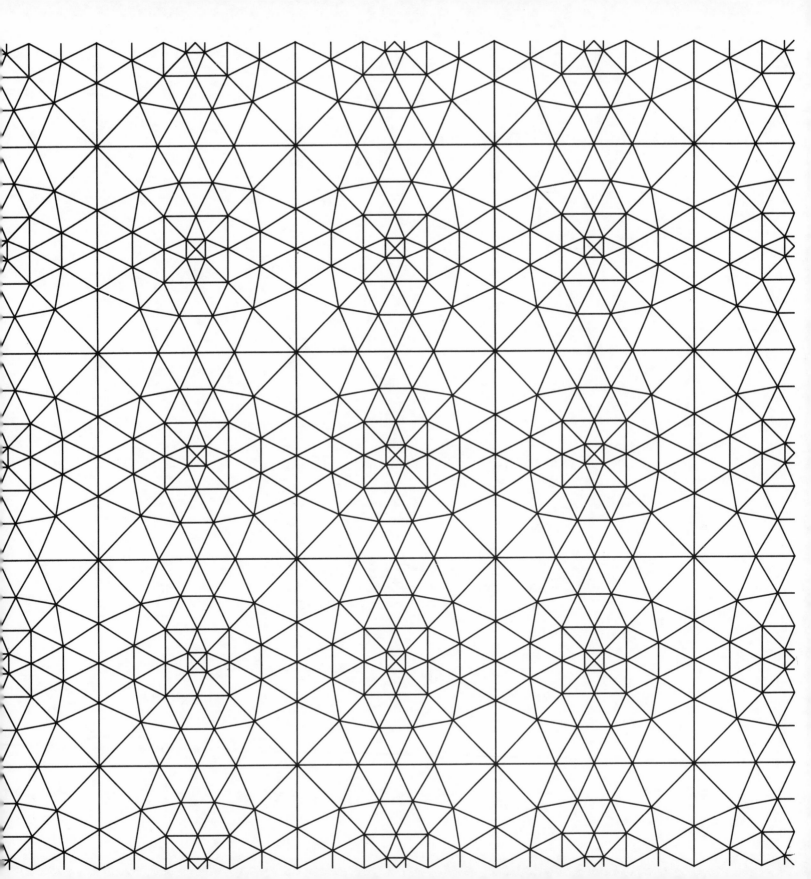

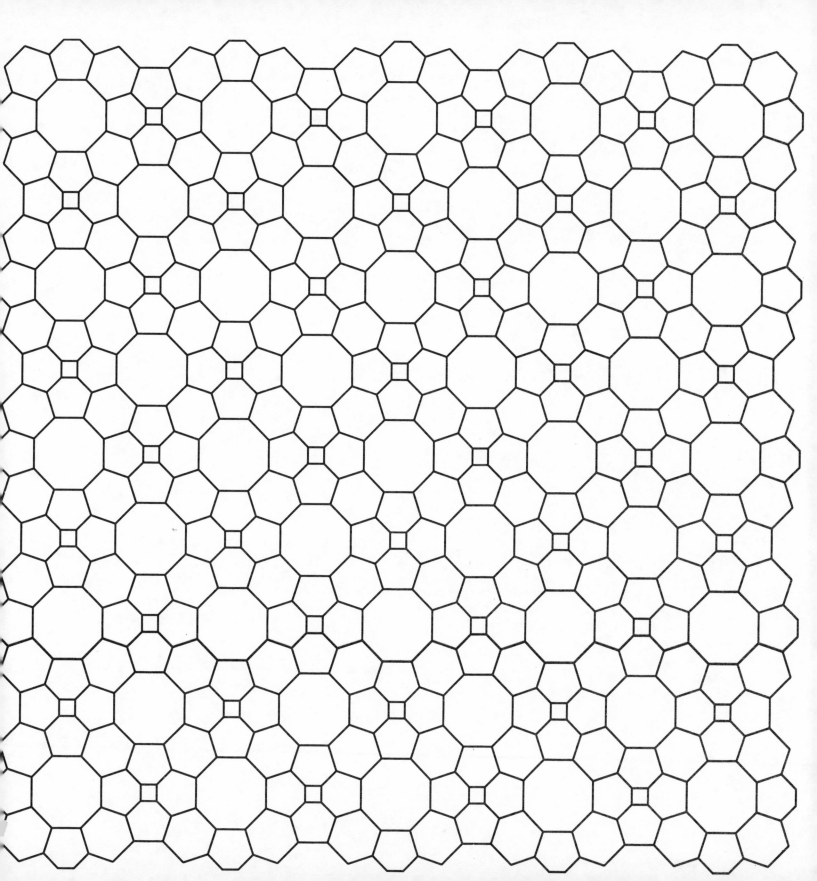

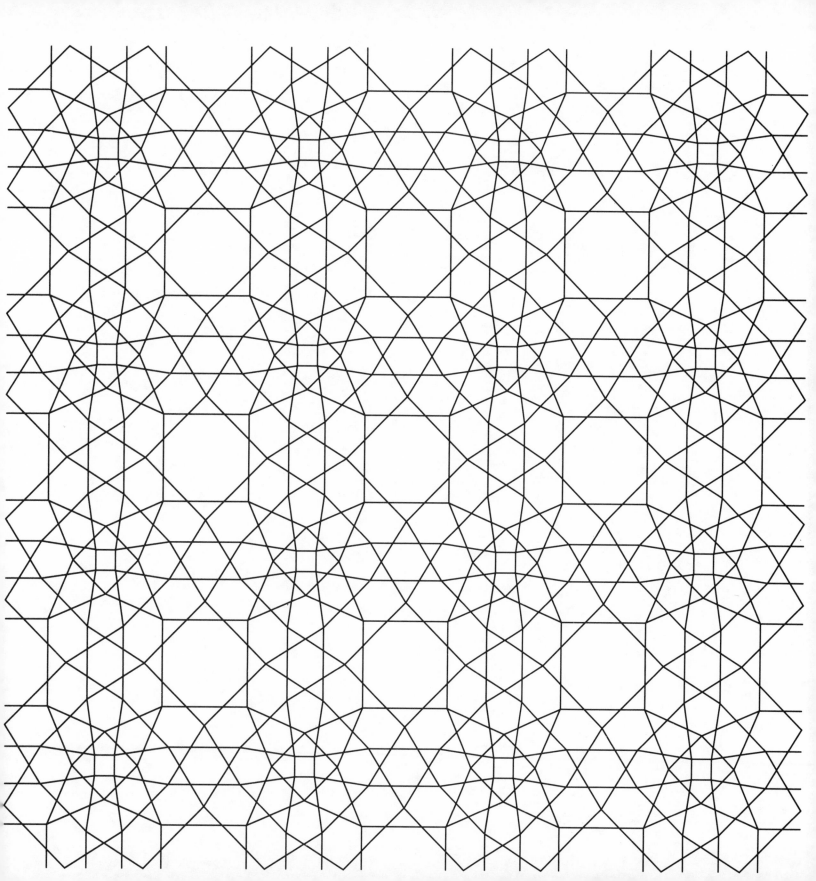

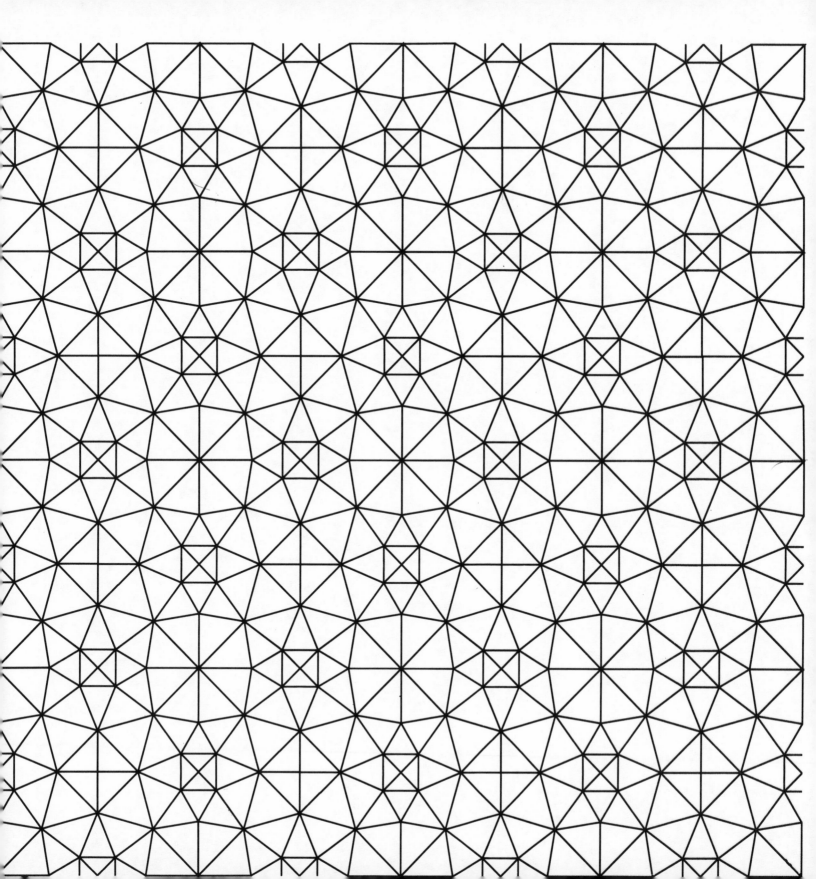

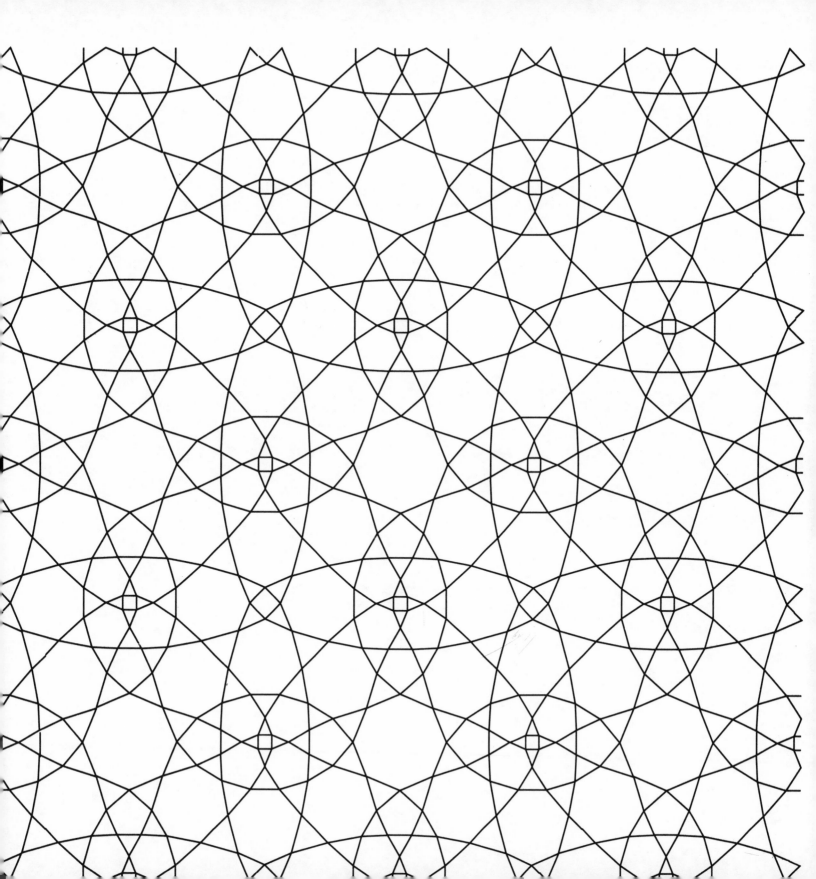

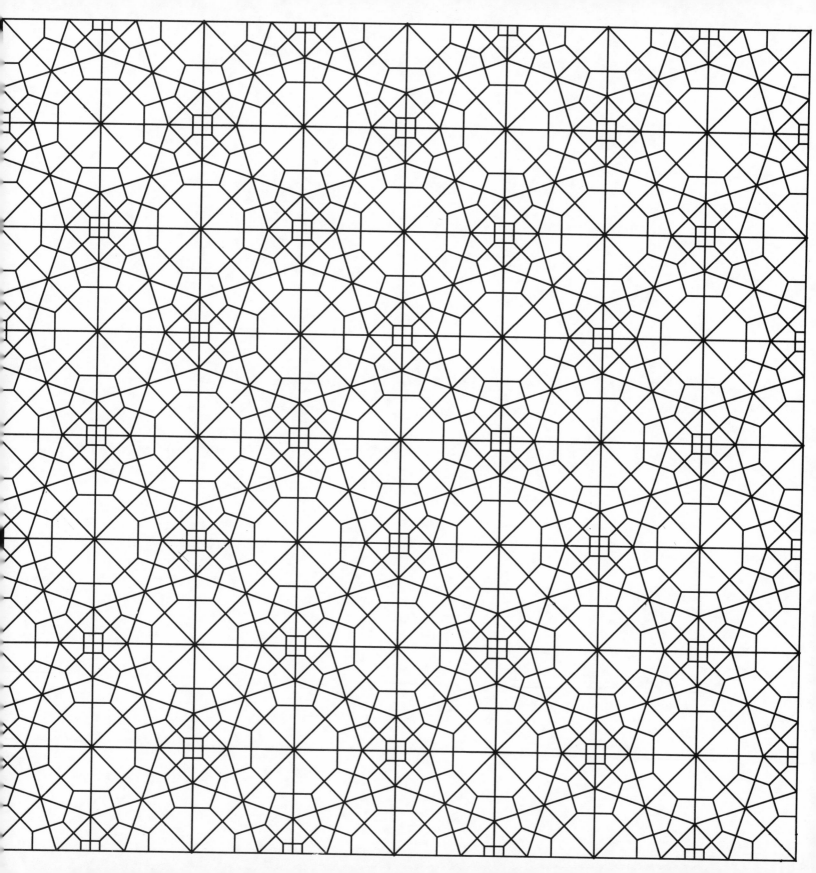

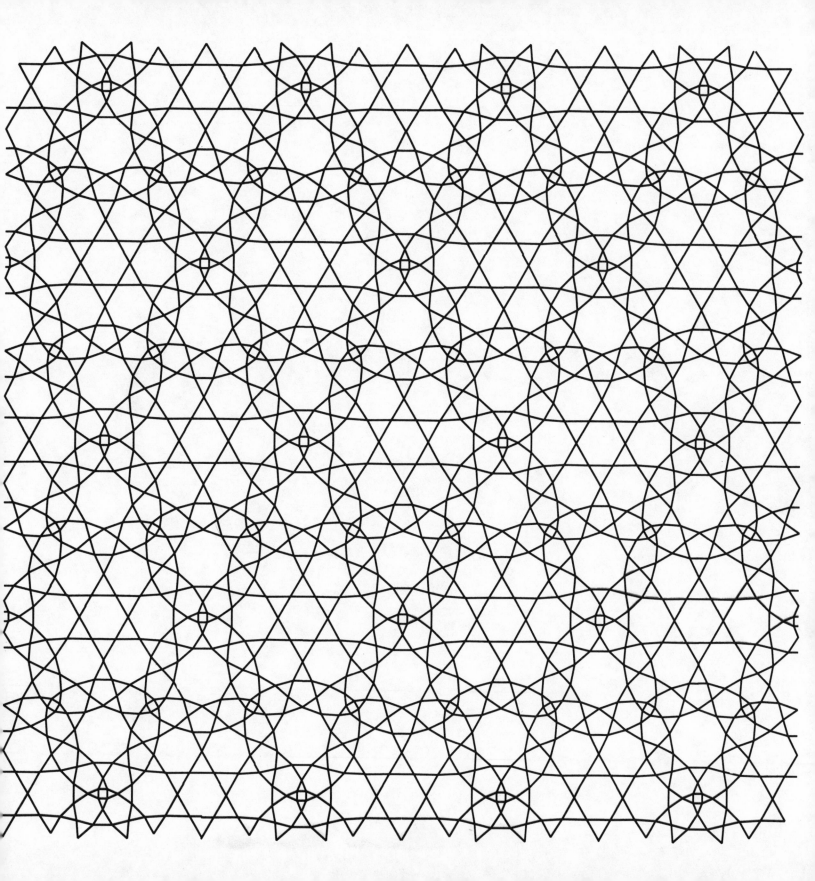

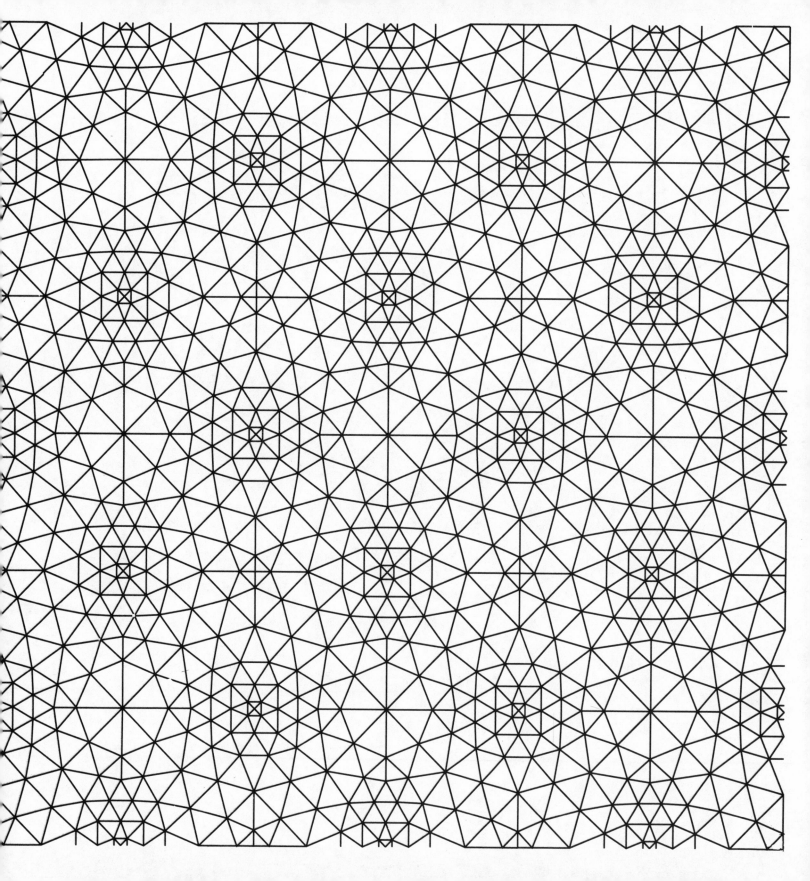

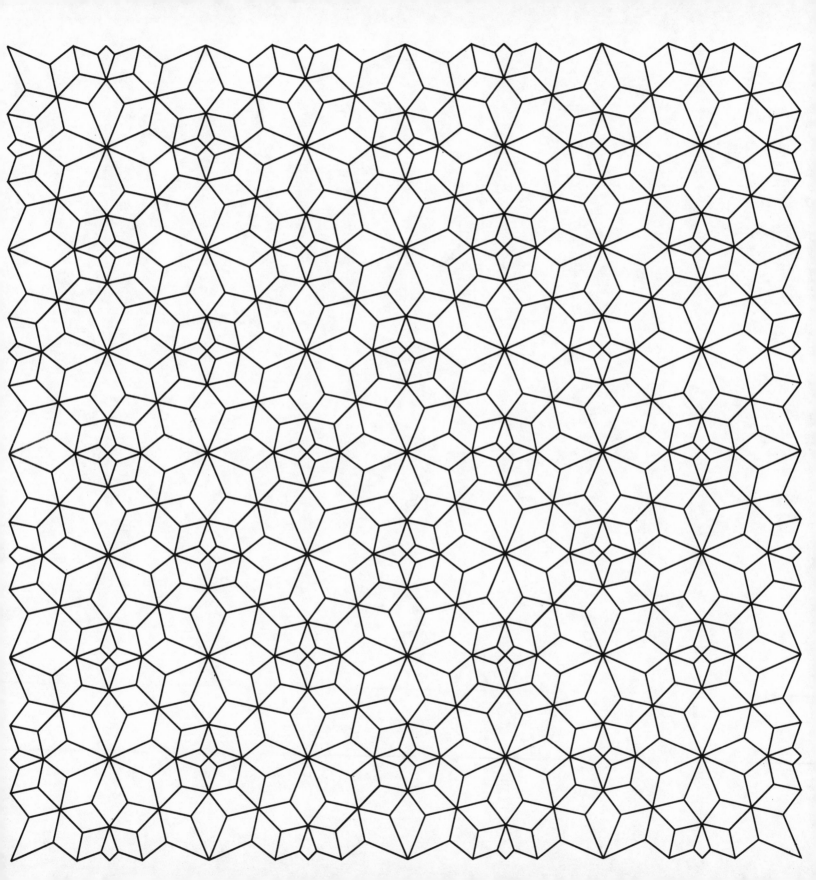

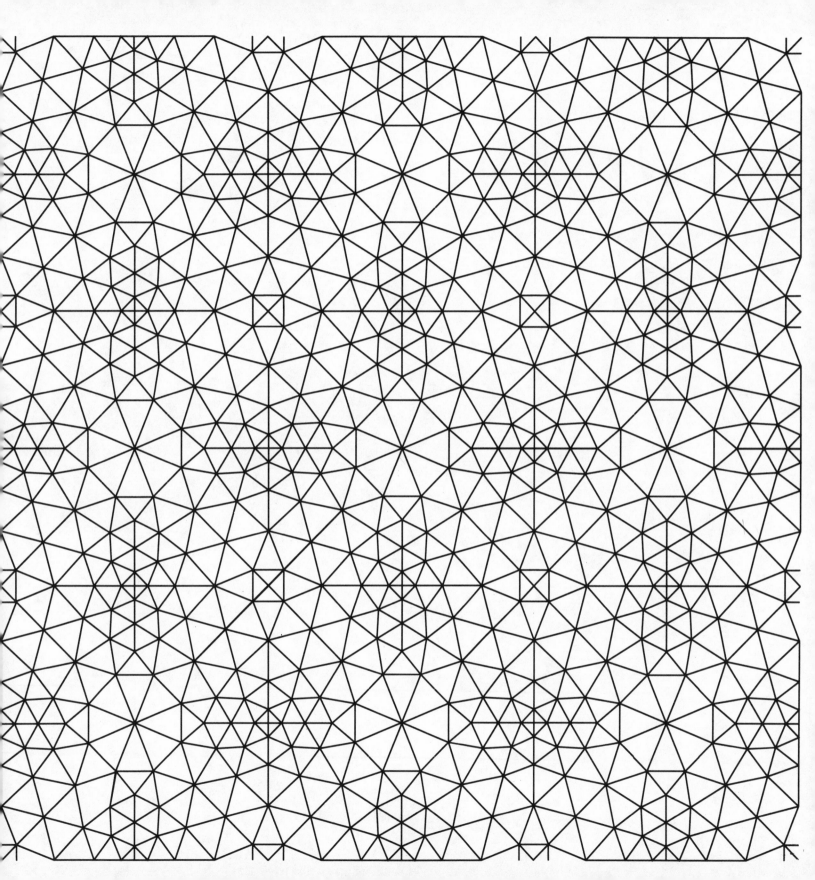

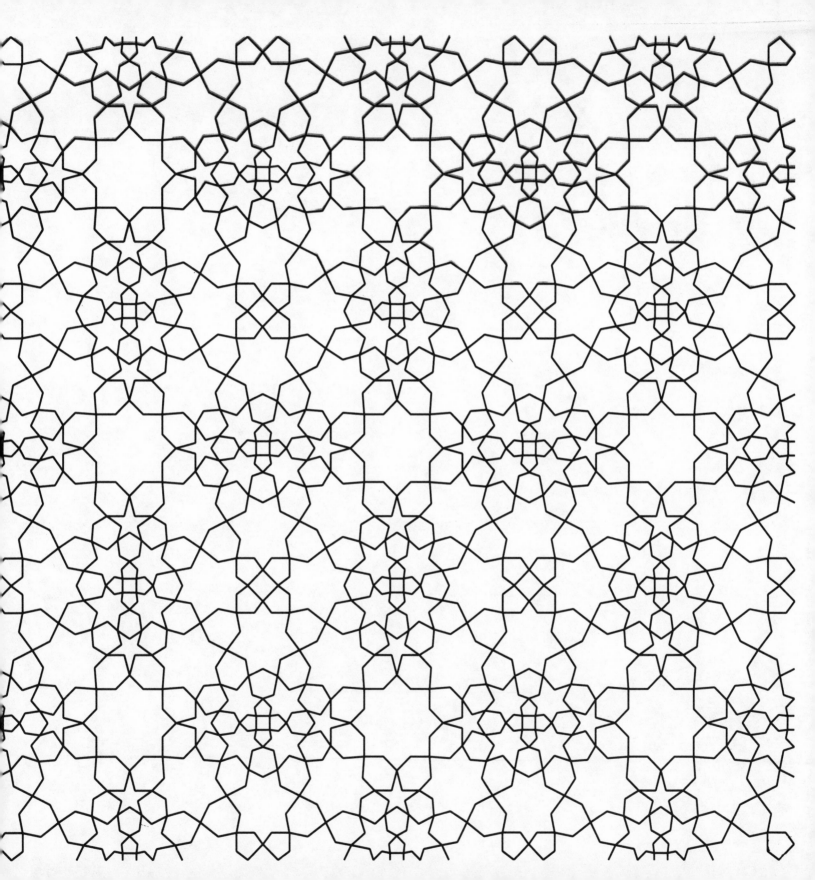

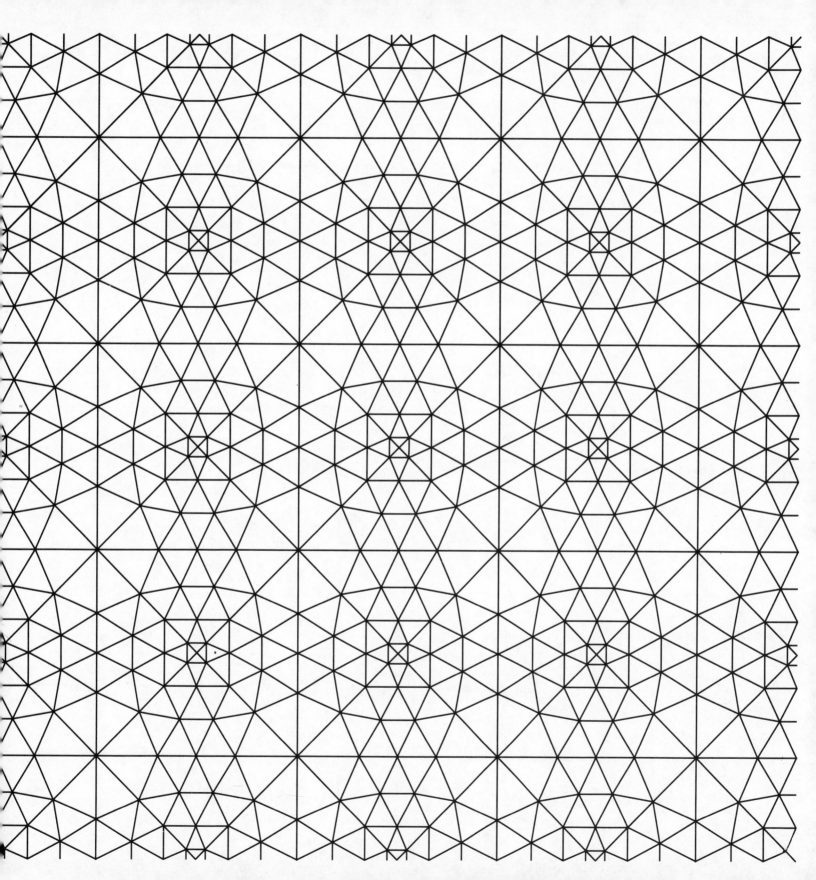

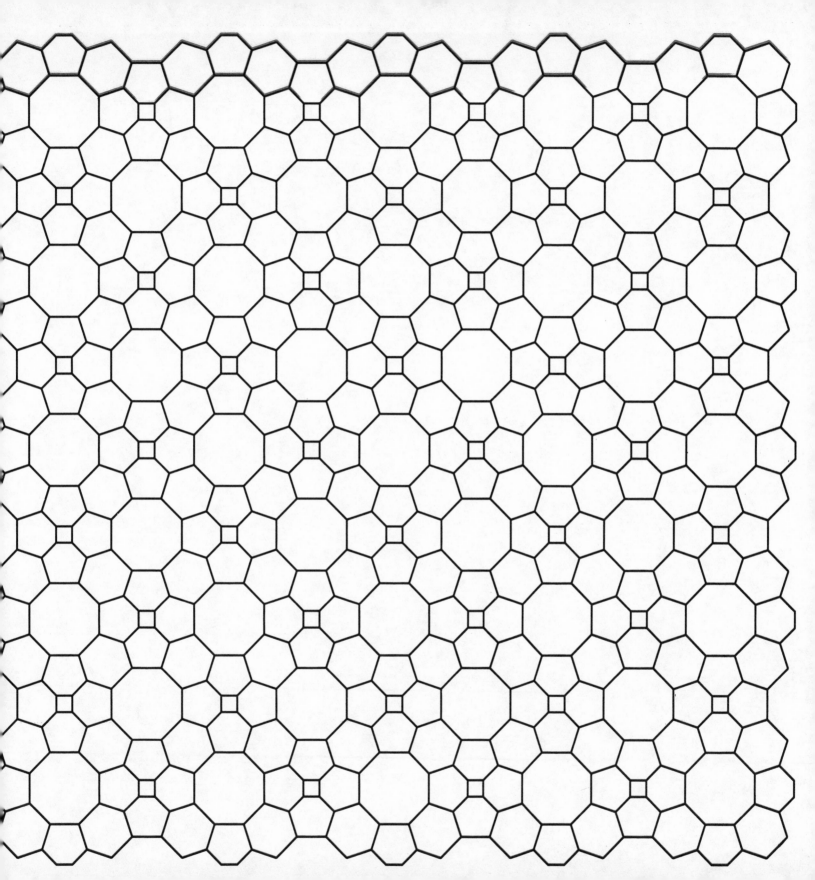

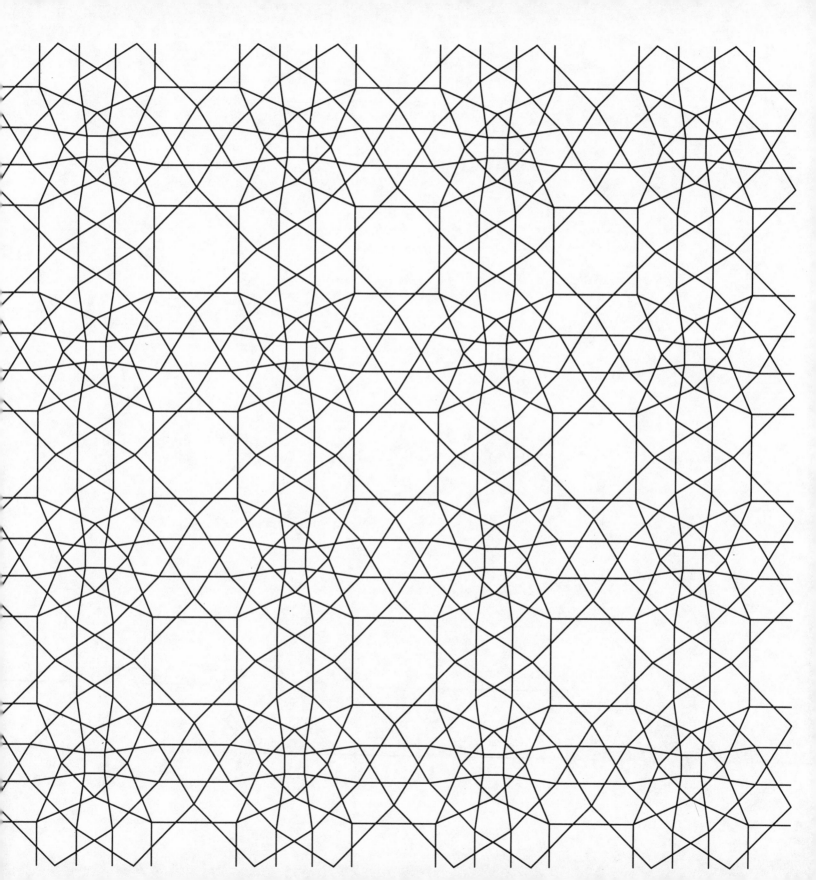

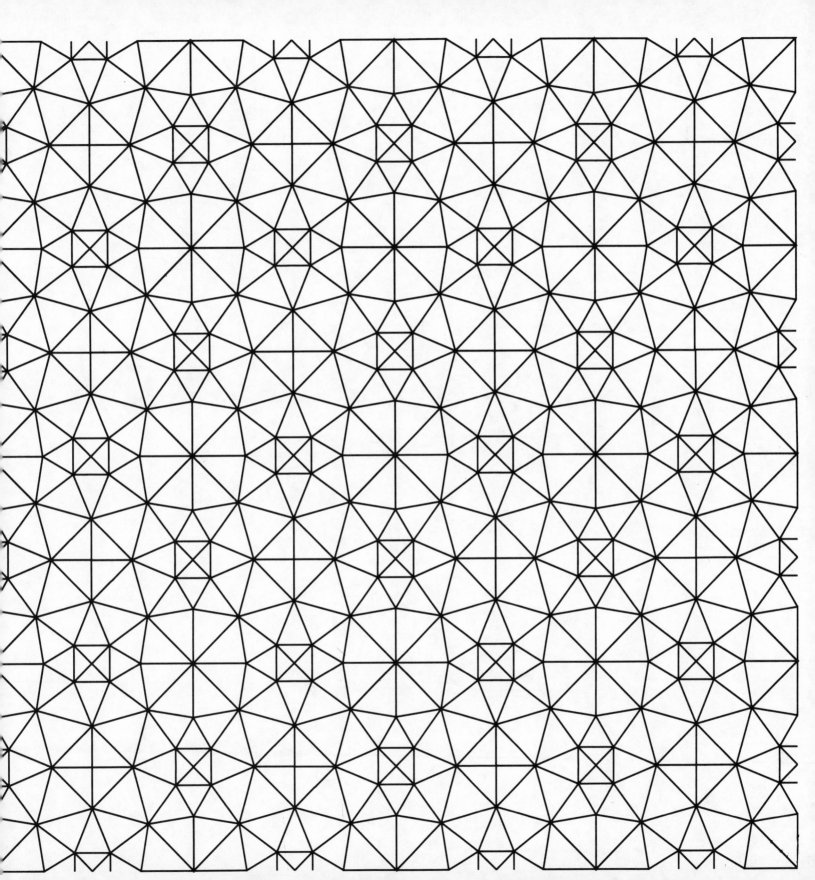

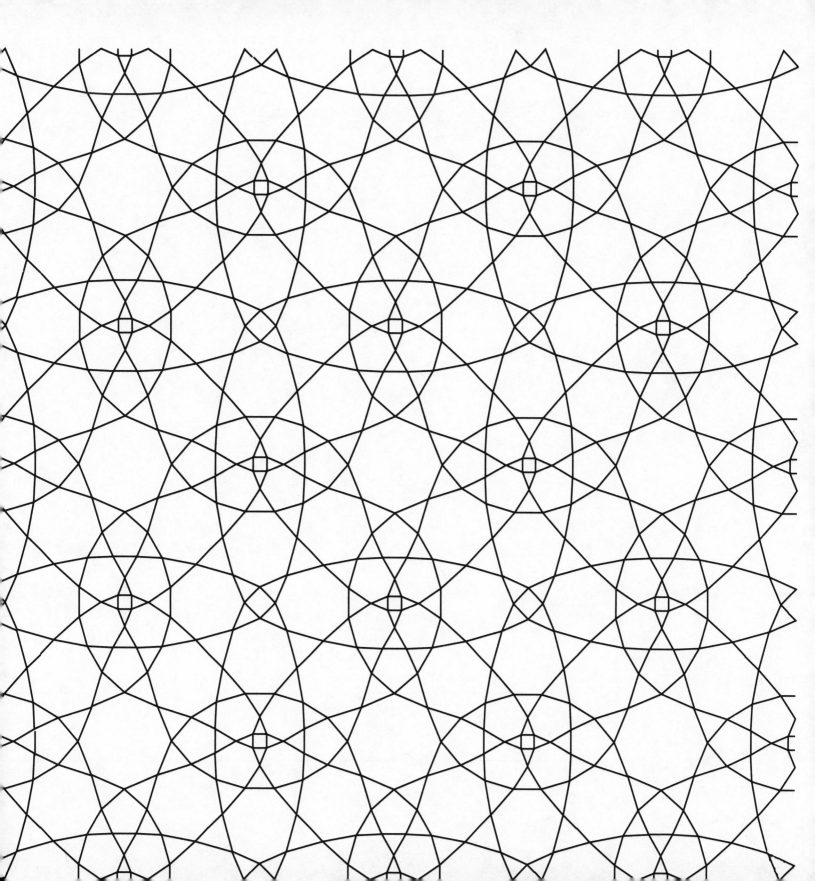

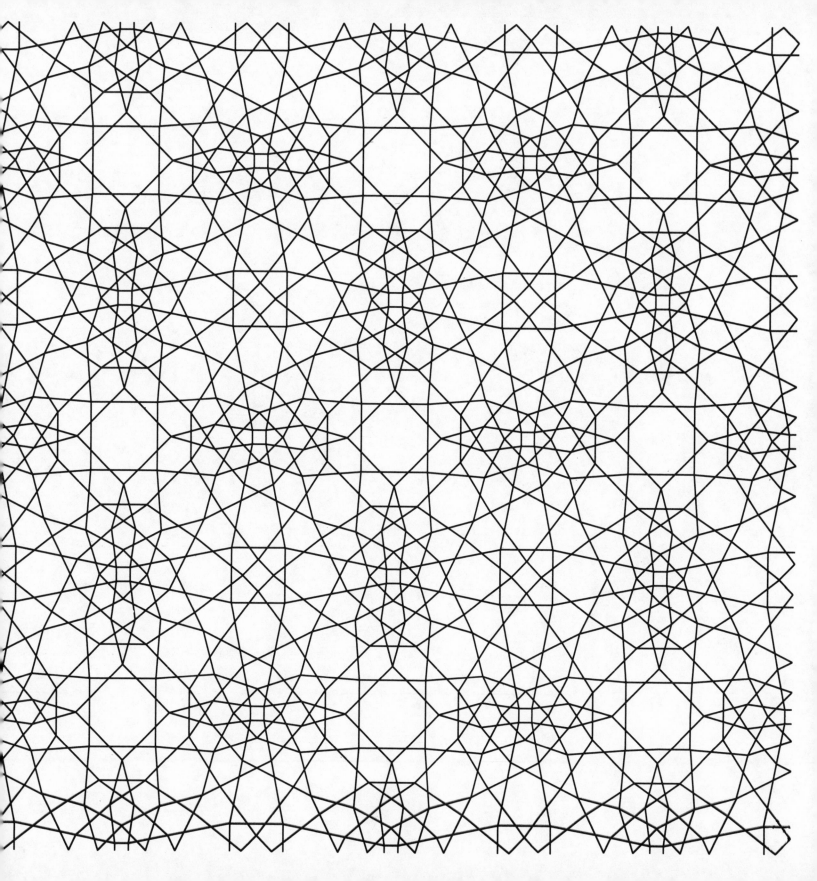

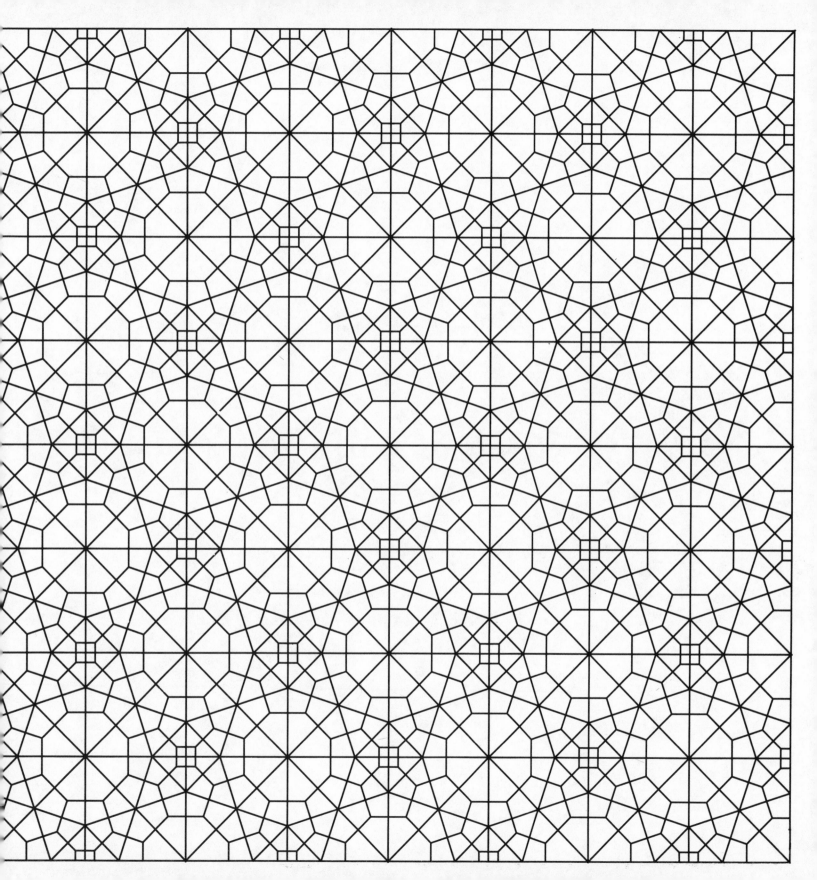

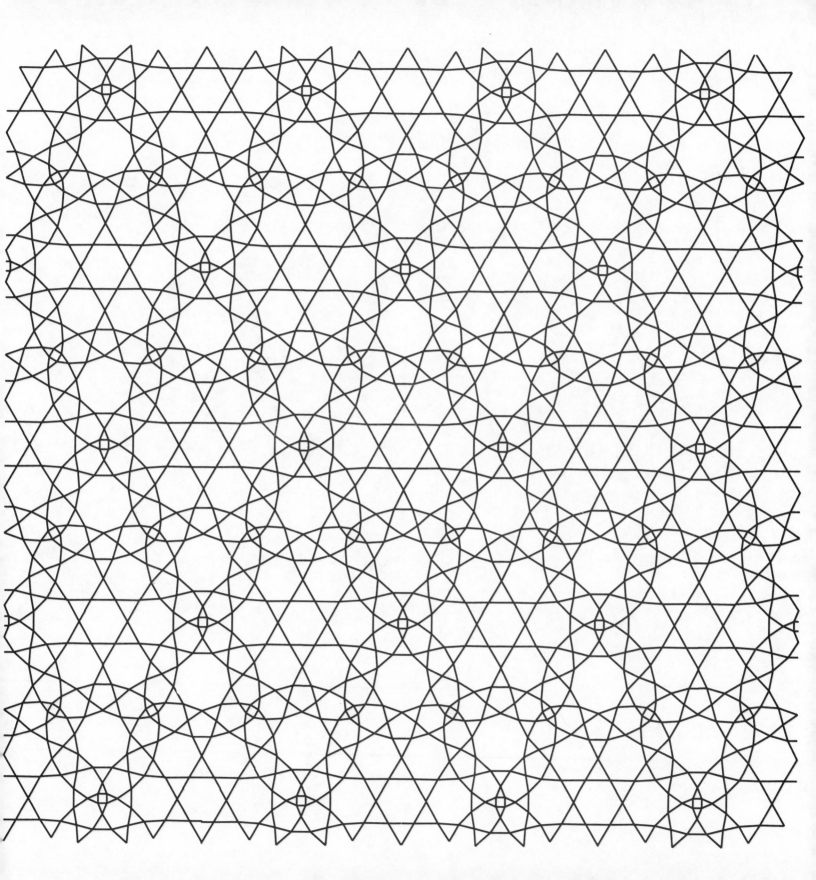

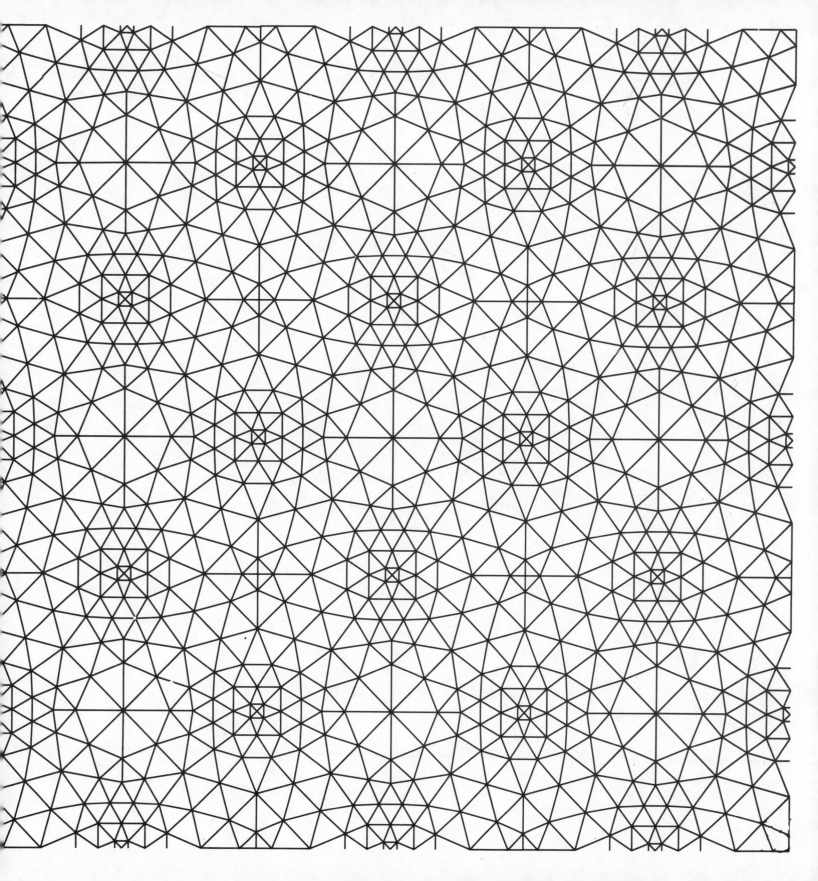

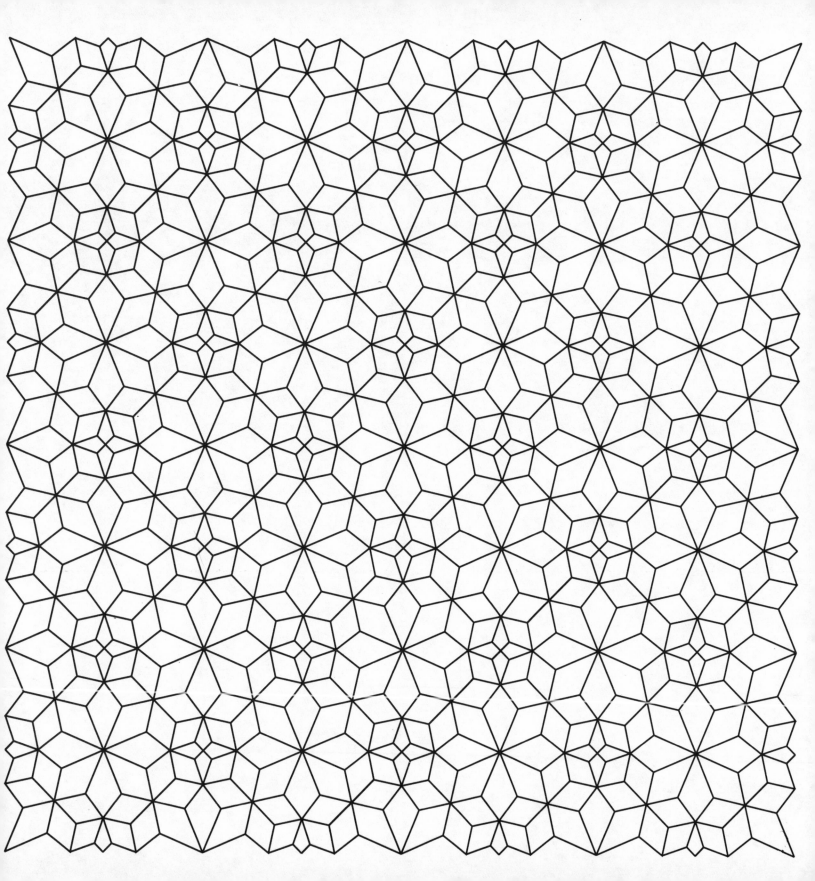

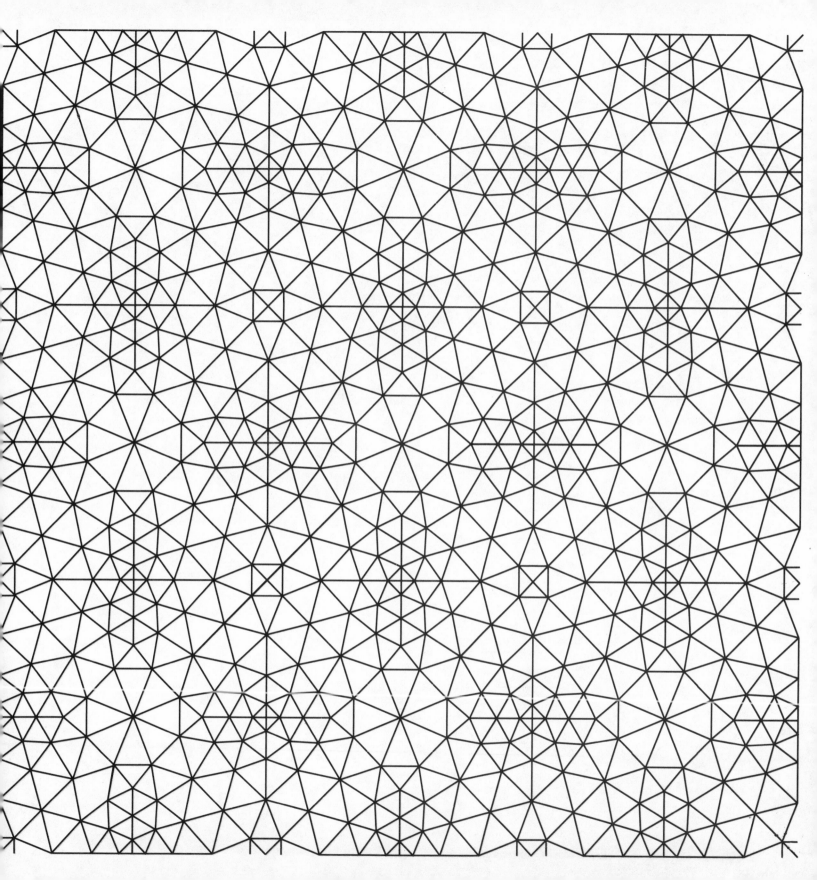

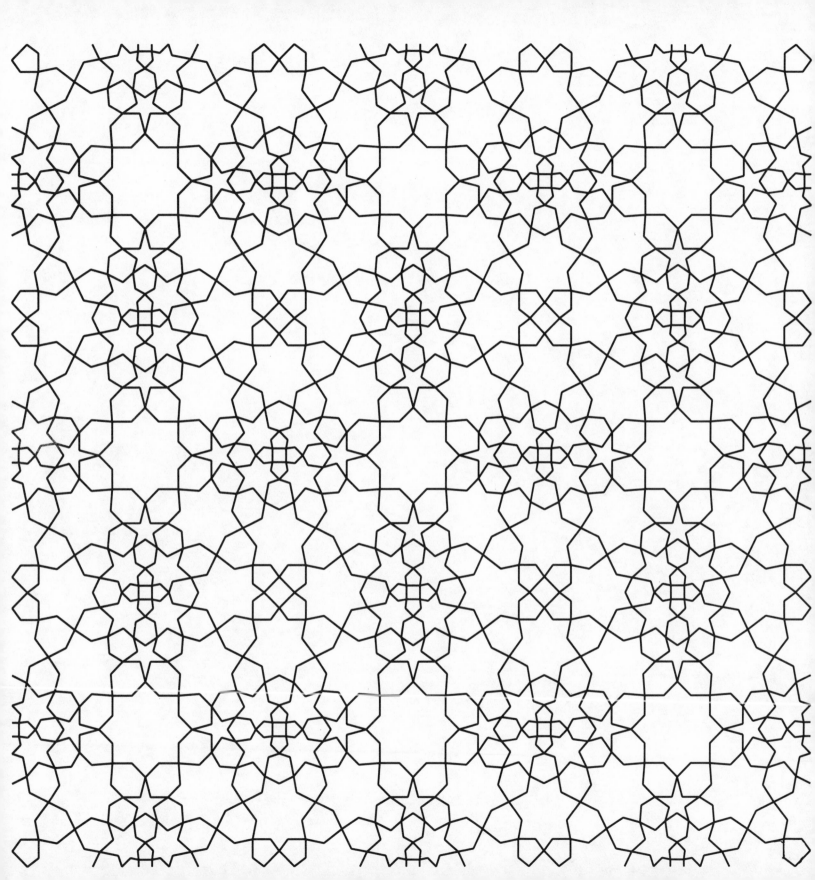

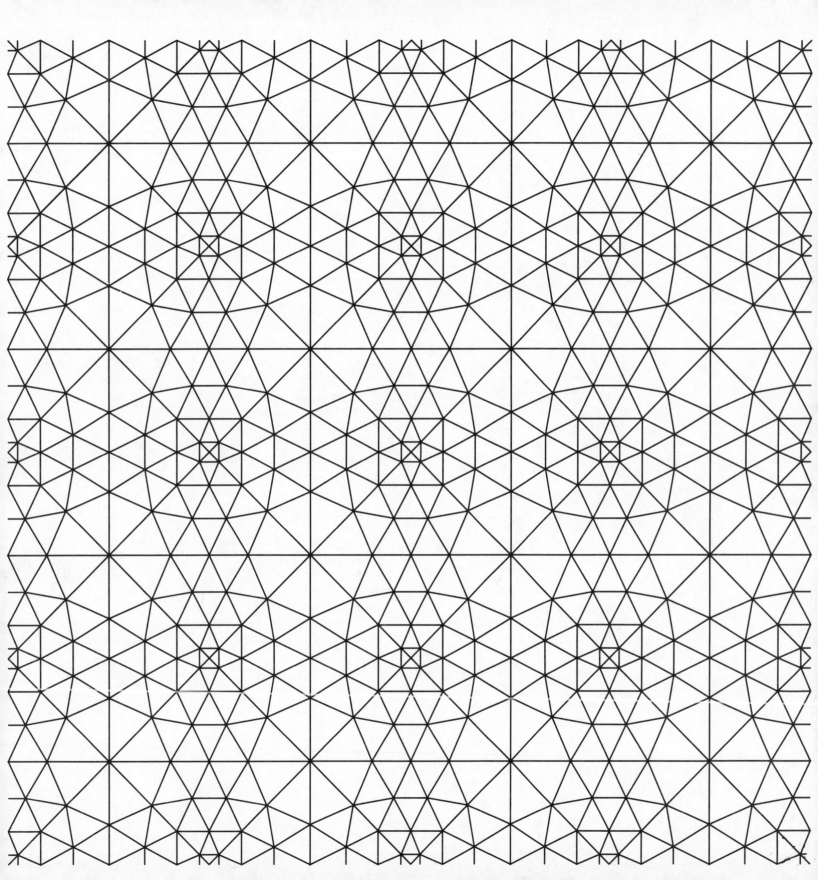

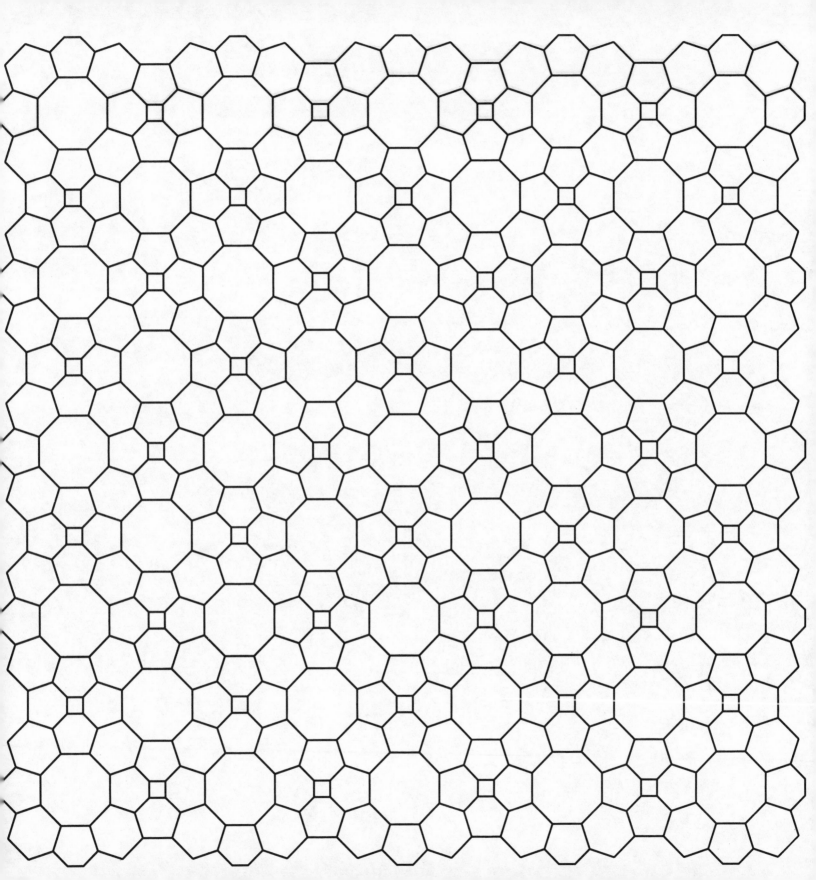

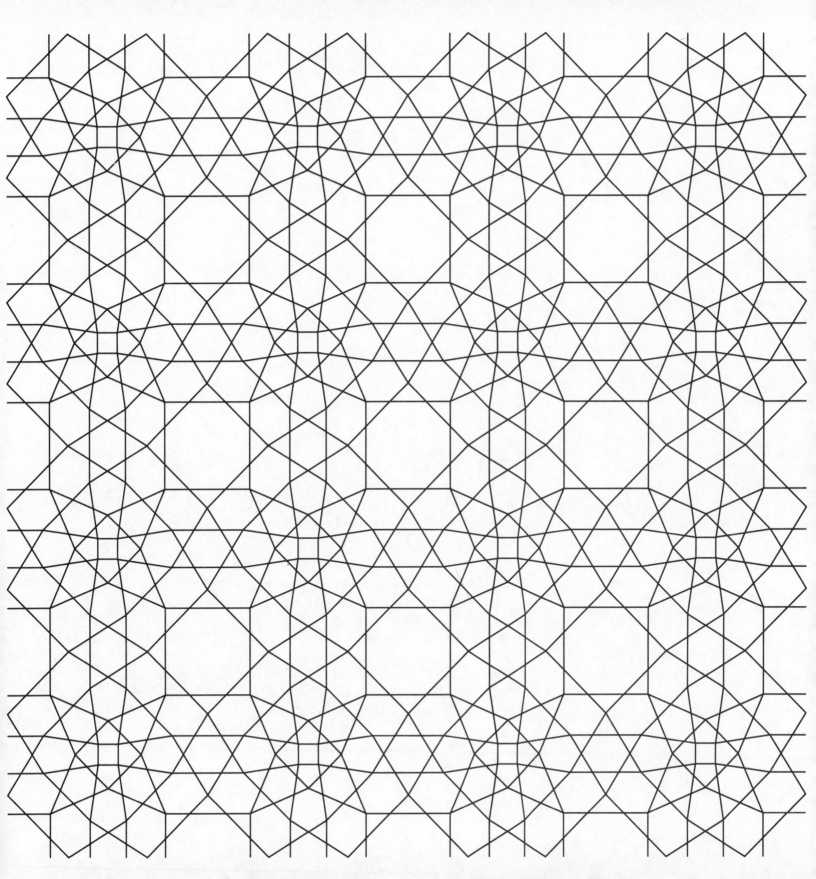

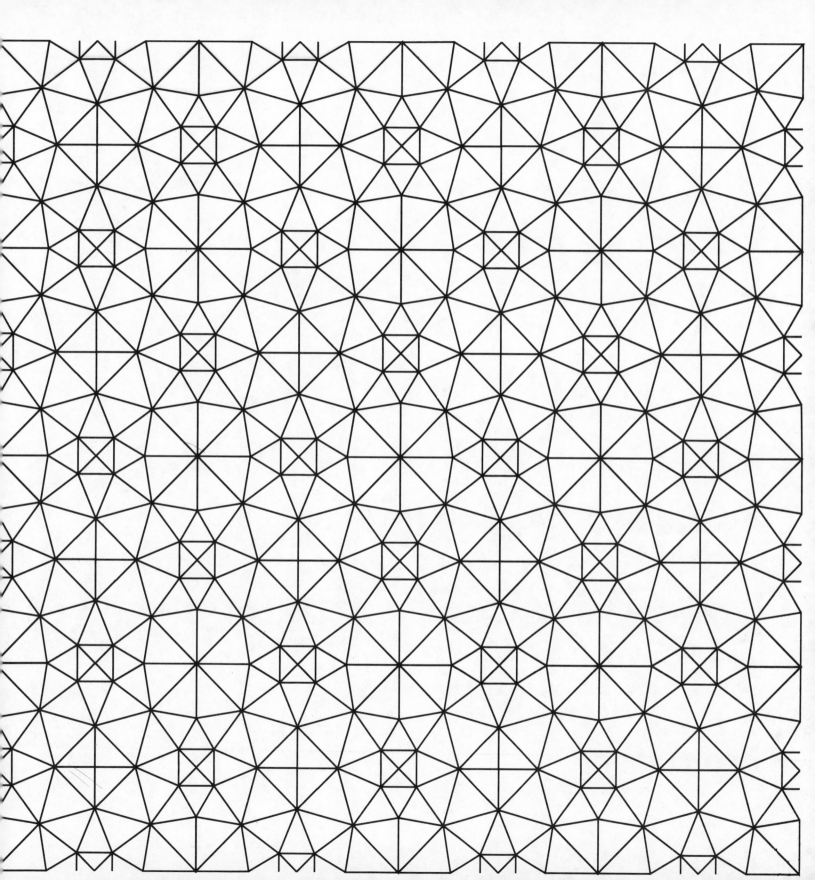

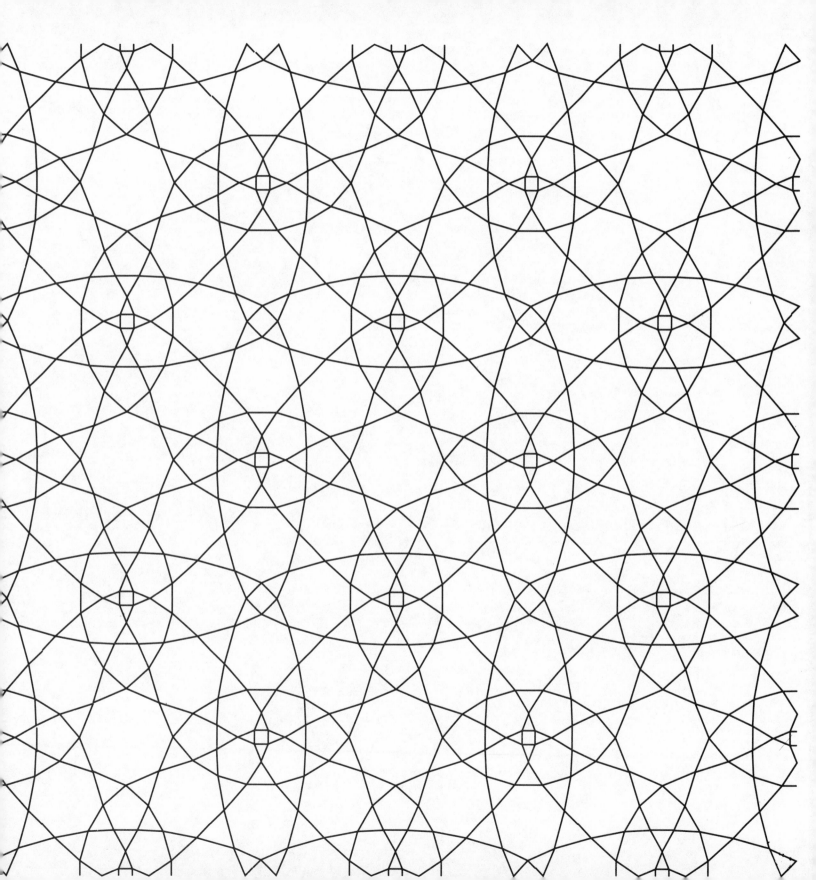

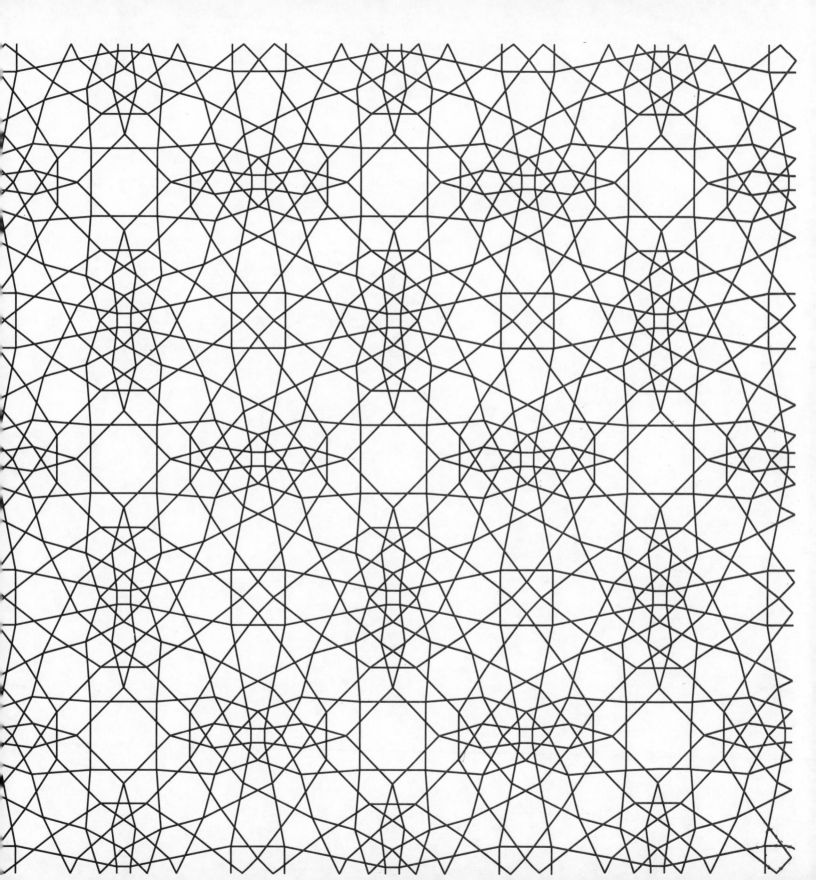

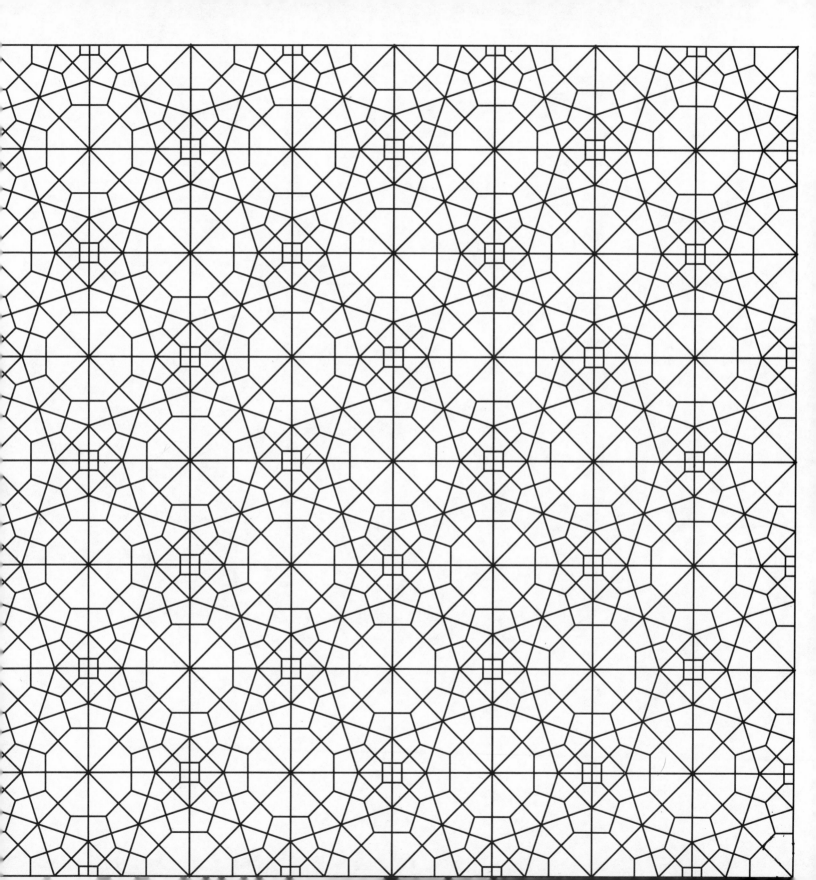

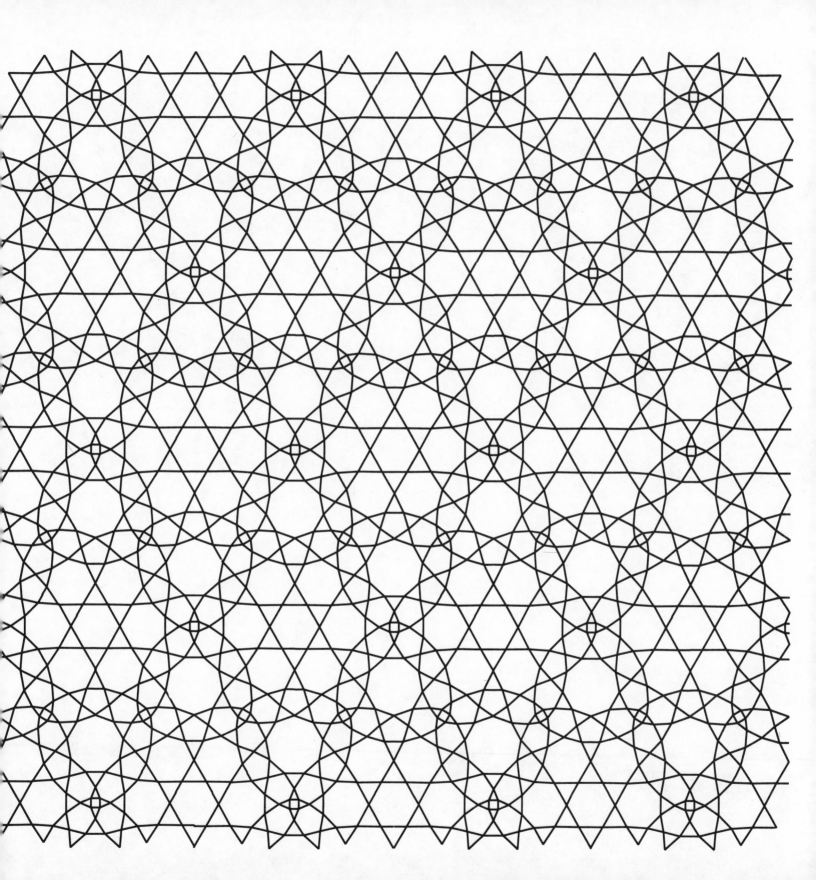

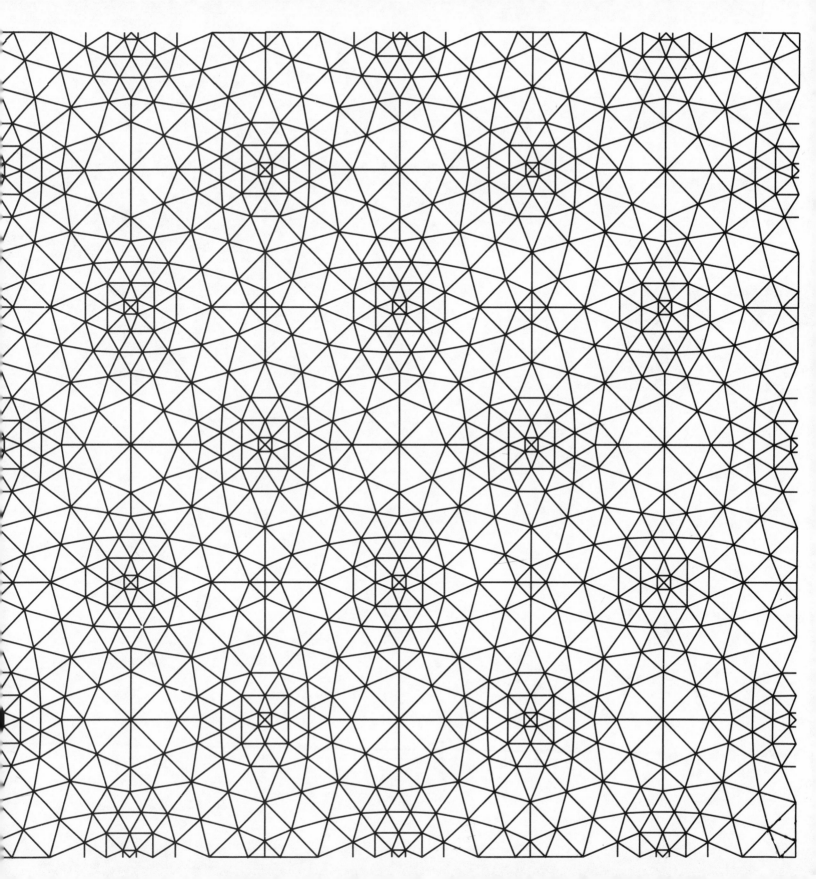